Dedication

I dedicate this little book to each of you who are waking up to, or are already experiencing the Journey of Conscious Creating!

My wish is that you find all that you seek and more as you discover just how amazing you truly are!
*Each one of us on this planet matters, **you** matter, so,*
Thank you!
For being exactly who you are!

Namaste'
Charley

Forward:

It is with great honor that I write a few words about this inspirational book. As a student of the Mind and of the Universe, I have come to find that there are certain irrefutable truths; these Laws of the Universe are the basis of the book. Charley Edwards has hit the cosmic "nail on the head" with this wonderful little book, Eleven Ways to Improve Your Life. He is able to drive home 11 points that if we all take time to study and learn, our lives will be increased.

The most powerful words in the Universe are "I AM" and Charley has taken those words and made a book which is simple and yet very complete. Everything is created in our thoughts and our ability to control and focus those thoughts, are paramount to our results, good or bad. If you don't like your results, go back and look at how they happened- it all started with a thought.

Enjoy this book. Study this book. There is much more to these few pages than the written word shows. Use the thoughts here to start your mind to thinking in a new direction with new thoughts.

This is a magical book that deserves your study and reflection, in it is a formula that if practiced will change your life- your creative thoughts can't help but give you the results you desire!

I AM Creator!

Namaste'

Jeff Mays
Training Coordinator
Bob Proctor's Life Success Consultants
www.jeffmays.us

I Am a Perfect

Part of Creation...

Contents

1. Have an Open Mind
2. Our Thoughts Become Our Reality
3. Become Aware of Your Thoughts
4. Create Strengthening Thinking Patterns
5. Overcoming Our Fears
6. Create a Dream, Create Your Life
7. Begin it!
8. Stretch Yourself
   Mind – Body – Spirit
9. Make the Commitment
10. Ask
11. Allow The Magic to Happen

I Am

abundance

我們是

We
Are
One...

Traditional Chinese

One

Have An Open Mind

For each of us to be in a place of
receiving new
information or knowledge
of any kind we must first
open our mind &
be willing to learn.
Every day is brand new and gift
wrapped for a child. Allow the child in
you to be curious about all things and
re-be an explorer of the world.

学会

Learn

Traditional Chinese

*We simply cannot be rigid
or inflexible with old patterns
of thinking
and expect to create new
results for ourselves.*

"One cannot solve a problem
with the same thinking that
created it."

Albert Einstein

We must be
open minded and
flexible to new ideas
if we truly desire
positive change in our
lives.

The definition of insanity is

Doing the same thing &

Expecting a different result!

Japanese Image

法官沒有

Judge Not

Traditional Chinese

We must,

if only for a short time,

suspend our thoughts

and feelings

of judgment

增長

Grow

Traditional Chinese

It is then

That We Begin

To Really Grow.

"Give yourself

Permission"

To try something new

And ask:

"What have

I got to gain?"

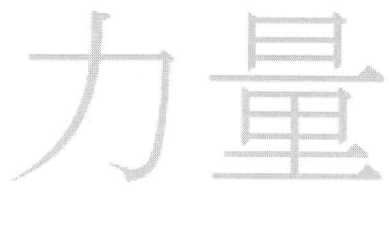

Strength

"It is in your moments of decision that your destiny is shaped."

Tony Robbins

Your wish is my command . . .

Two

Our Thoughts

& Feelings

Become

Our Reality...

It may sound strange or even sound crazy to you; I know it did to me the first time I heard this. I really had to stretch my mind!

It is our own thoughts and feelings that are the tools we use to create

Our own results,

Our own reality!

想象

Imagine

Simplified Chinese

Quantum science suggests that our thoughts and feelings are simply a form of energy and we are the transmitters of the signal; the energy that travels out to the universe 24/7.

It is that energy that is the asking in "Ask and you will receive"

"What you think about, you bring about"

"What we focus on really does expand"

Pay attention to what your mind is focused on most of the time and you will soon see that you are attracting even more of whatever that is. . .

Change your thoughts and you will change your reality, it's a law of the Universe, the Law of Attraction!!

It really is that simple!

I Am...

Harmony

我以為

I Am

Thought

Traditional Chinese

Three

Become Aware Of Your Thoughts

Our thoughts are sometimes conscious and sometimes subconscious. The subconscious thoughts are often quiet inner feelings about a thing more than a voice in our head.

It is our subconscious thoughts and beliefs that control all our behaviours and actions.

By becoming aware of those beliefs we give ourselves
    "Conscious choice"
As we consciously choose our thoughts, feelings and actions we truly experience being free . . .

We are not helpless victims of life. We are the co-creators of every minute of our lives. Most of us are simply doing this unconsciously. That's where the phrase "stuff happens" comes from. Becoming a "Conscious Creator" is a key to living the life of our dreams and experiencing true freedom!

I Am a...

神志清楚

Conscious

创作者

Creator

Simplified Chinese

選択

Choice

Japanese

In order to create success in our lives we must become aware; become conscious of the subconscious thoughts we have;
This is our self-talk.

Our self talk is that sometimes not so quiet voice we hear in our head, and most often it says negative things about us like: "Oh, that was dumb", "what's wrong with me anyways?" or "Will I ever be good enough?"

After countless repetitions, it is those messages forming a habitual thought pattern of self blame, which in time, becomes a limiting self-concept or belief which then becomes firmly rooted in your subconscious mind.

*Once we become aware of the messages or negative thought patterns our self-talk is sending us, we are able to change those messages into more empowering ones if we choose to. These new messages of success after many repetitions will soon become our new and healthier self-concept; our new self-created habit of thought. Just imagine being able to "choose" who you are instead of simply believing what others have said about you. When will you choose to select your **own opinion** of yourself over the one someone else has offered?*

自已
采纳

I Am
Self
Respect

Simplified Chinese

Four

Create Strengthening Thinking Patterns

Strength

Simplified Chinese

Our subconscious thoughts control our actions; therefore, when we begin to become aware of our negative self-messages, it is our responsibility to change our inner messages to more strengthening thinking patterns about ourselves.

One key to learning is

<u>Repetition</u>

Just as the negative messages we have heard many times have become our belief system or self concept, we can also reprogram our mental hard drive with new empowering messages using

<u>Affirmations!</u>

Our emotions are the "super glue" that turns affirmations into reality.

Affirmations

+ Emotions

+ Repetition

= Change

When repeating new messages many times over, we begin to observe changes taking place in our own behaviour. With only a little more effort comes the commitment to follow the formula for change.

~

Repetitions plus Affirmations plus Emotions; now you're creating change consciously!

Always make your affirmations in present time language, for example:

*I am _____. Or,
I love having _____.
If you want something in your present, you must think, feel and speak of it "as if" it already exists in your present.
"Fake it 'til you make it!"*

As we do the repetitions, we build a pathway in our brain just like walking through the woods creates a path. Once the path is consciously created, our brain will follow it automatically!

All it takes is repetitions of a message -- so get started!

I Am

道路

The Path...

Five

Overcoming Our Fears

Courage is not the absence of fear, but the ability to take action in spite of it.

Anthony Robbins

*Many of us believe that those people who are getting the greatest results in life rarely experience fear; this is an illusion! Everyone attempting to do something new experiences fear at some time. The only difference between those we view as very successful and those who are not is this; Those who are successful experience the fear but they don't allow it to immobilize them, they use that energy to motivate them into **taking action!***

They feel the fear but they do it anyway, not allowing their fear to stop them from creating their dreams. You can too! All you have to do is "decide" from deep within yourself that the fear won't stop you! Whether you decide you can't do something or whether you decide you can *do something is your choice*

You're right!

So why not decide right now that,

You Can!

Everything is possible!

Simply notice the fear and then pass right through it like any other illusion.

Illusion

"As we are liberated from our own fear, our presence automatically liberates others"

Nelson Mandela

我自由

I Am

Freedom

Traditional Chinese

梦想

I Am the

Dream...

Simplified Chinese

Six

Create a Dream
Create a Life

To fantasize or *Dream Big* is something most of us were taught *not* to do as children, yet people who have fantasized are the ones who have created the greatest changes in our world.

The Wright Brothers, Walt Disney and Oprah Winfrey are all people who started with only a fantasy.

A *Dream* or vision of what could be. Then, they set out to create the results they fantasized about.

"Dream big and then

grow yourself

into the dream"

"Dream lofty dreams, and as you

dream, so shall you become."

James Allen

开始

Begin

I Am the Beginning...

Simplified Chinese

Seven

Begin It!

What ever your dream is,
begin it!
Where you are, with what
you have!
Then the Universe will
support you fully!

Successful people do not pay attention to the current facts or results they are getting. They do not allow those facts to be their reality but instead just a place they are passing through to their Success.

The facts or results in your life are simply the results of yesterday's thoughts and feelings. No matter what the current facts are in your life, begin your dream today.

In whatever capacity you are presently able. Begin, do and think things that will bring you closer to your dream.

Do one thing a day no matter how large or how small towards your dream

&

Some day you will have it. The universe begins to move automatically to bring you all you need as you step forward with courage and faith.

Start volunteer work,

Work part time,

Whatever you can do,

Begin it NOW!

"Opportunity is missed by most people because it is dressed in overalls and looks like work".

Thomas Edison

I Am

机会

Opportunity

Opportunity is around us 24/7. Learning to recognize an opportunity can change your life in seconds.

Most people focus their mind on the problem they must overcome instead of focusing on the lesson which teaches them more about themselves; this teaching can help us to understand where it is we don't allow the wonderful gifts of life to come to us.

Changing our focus from the problem to the solution is the key and this may require us to stretch our mind out of our habitual ways of thinking.

As uncomfortable as it can be, stretching is a good thing!

伸張

Stretch

Japanese

Eight

Stretch Your Self

Mind ∂ Body ∂ Spirit

Most people read an average of one book a year. If we were to read one book a month, we would be stretching our minds and improving our lives. Wisdom is personal power!

We must think of our bodies as our vehicles. If we want our car to run smoothly we must keep it properly maintained. The same is true for our bodies. We must do some form of physical activity each day; eat nourishing foods and get good rest to properly maintain our bodies.

Spirit is our essence. We must a take few minutes of quiet time each day to connect with our soul-self; this greatly enhances our creativity and helps keep us calm through life's challenges.

"All of man's miseries derive from not being able to sit quietly in a room alone."

17th century scientist,
Blaise Pascal

犯

Commit;

I Am Commitment...

Simplified Chinese

Nine

Commitment is not a dirty word...

Commitment is one of the keys we can use to grow ourselves.

In order for our lives to change and become the life of our dreams, we must make a commitment to ourselves to do whatever inner growth is required to achieve the results we truly desire.

Whether you want to be a ditch digger, a doctor, a teacher or whatever, you must first commit to doing that which is required. If we want to travel the world or build a business, we must find out what to do and be willing to do what is required.

There are only two questions you must ask yourself

"Am I capable?"

*Yes you are!
If you can learn;
you can learn how!*

&

"Am I willing?"

*To do whatever
inner growth is required?*

Make the commitment;

Make it happen!

Making it happen does not mean to force it. When we push against things, they tend to push back or create resistance. Making it happen is simply doing the repetitions required to shift a belief or paradigm from something that limits your success to something that enhances your success.

要

Traditional Chinese

Ten

Ask

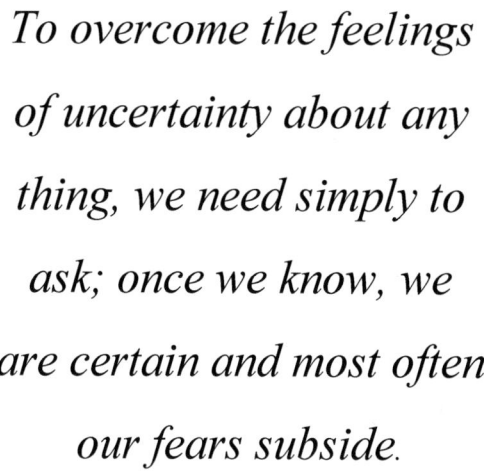

To overcome the feelings of uncertainty about any thing, we need simply to ask; once we know, we are certain and most often our fears subside.

Many of us have a deep fear of looking silly or being judged by others and therefore choose not to ask for help or information. Instead, we stumble around in pain and fear trying to figure things out without any support from others.

Why re-invent the wheel?

The only silly question is the one we don't ask. We must accept that some people will laugh at us if we ask.

Some will scoff,
some will call us names,
but more importantly,
we will then know the answer to our question, and knowledge gives us choices!

Neale Donald Walsh, Oprah and Wayne Dyer are examples of successful people who have experienced being laughed at, made fun of and called names. Instead of allowing this to immobilize them and stop their dreams from becoming reality, they continued asking questions that would assist their learning and growth.

Through this journey of personal development each of them has grown into whom they've chosen to be.
Be willing to ask questions. Seek and you shall find!
Ask even if you think the questions are dumb!
One day you will find that others are asking you!

魔術

I AM

Magic

Traditional Chinese

Allow the Magic To Happen

When I say "allow" the magic to happen, what exactly does this mean?

What is the difference between making it happen and "allowing" it to happen?

Let's explore that some...

The only walls that block our success are the walls that we have built ourselves. The walls are simply made of the beliefs we carry that limit our success.

We have to get out of our own way and allow the magic to flow to us with ease.

Allowing the magic to flow to us greatly improves our lives.

We might think, feel and say things like "Oh, I could never have that" or "Ya, that's easy for you!"

This kind of statement only implies an inner belief or program that says "it is not easy for you" which is really just a wall you've created yourself with thoughts. These thoughts block what you really want from coming into your present; The Now! There are no thoughts in your mind that you do not put there, so choose the good ones!

By creating and repeating positive affirmations as many times a day as you can, coupled with the super glue of emotions, you will remove and reprogram the blocks that stand between you and your dream life. You will be getting out of your own way and allowing the magic to come to you.

*Becoming aware of the walls or beliefs that block your success gives you the choice to change them, if you choose to. By changing the beliefs that say "I can't" into "I am" you will be allowing success to flow to you effortlessly.
Believe it, and you will see it!*

*"I can't" simply means,
"I don't yet know how",
and you can learn to if you choose to.
"Everything is possible"*

<u>*Affirmation:*</u>
I keep moving forward on my journey and growing through my life experiences with grace and humility.

真実

I Am

Truth...

Japanese

Closing Affirmation

I acknowledge that I am a part of something far greater than I am alone. I am a cell in the body of something much bigger than I am.

I am but a grain of sand, yet when I stand along side my brothers and sisters as humankind, we are the beach.

I Am

Peace

What ever you say,

    Inside or outside of your mind,

        After the words "I AM…"

            You Will Become…

I Am a Conscious Creator...

Author

C S Edwards

Charley S Edwards is a Certified Life Coach/Facilitator, published author/columnist and motivational speaker. He currently operates a retreat facility called Creating Room to Breathe, which is located in the quiet hamlet of Hawarden, Saskatchewan, Canada. There, he provides group and individual private coaching where he shares the principles of how to practice consciously creating a life of abundance and inner calm. These are the things he has learned and wishes to share with you so that you may have and enjoy more of the things in life that you really want!

Charley S Edwards also works with colleges, schools, non-profit organizations and many First Nations communities throughout the province of Saskatchewan.

Contact Charley S Edwards

www.creatingroomtobreathe.com

Phone: 306-855-2032

Or

Write to:

Box 178 Hawarden, SK

S0H 1Y0

Thank you for reading and searching;

Keep going!

Namasté

"I honor the place in you where there is only
One of us"

Charley

Acknowledgement

A huge thank you goes out to each of you whom have been my teachers along the path of this incredible journey.

It would take a whole other book to acknowledge each of you by name but I think you know who you are.
Thank you!

I Am grateful...

Thank you for reading "Eleven Little Ways to Improve Your Life" I appreciate you!

Come visit me on the net & sign up to receive my free newsletter "Living Satori" And join me on facebook.

<u>www.creatingroomtobreathe.com</u>

C S Edwards
Box 178 Hawarden, SK
S0H 1Y0

Retreat Facility: 1-306-855-2032

Call now to book your *free* one hour session to discover if *Life Coaching* is a fit for you:

Begin Living Your Best Life Today!

ISBN #: 978-0-557-80511-2

© 2010 All rights reserved.

Affirmations & Notes

Affirmations & Notes

Affirmations & Notes

Affirmations & Notes

Affirmations & Notes

Affirmations & Notes

Affirmations & Notes